Introducti

No-Knead Turbo Bread

Ready to Bake in 2-1/2 Hours

No Mixer... No Dutch Oven... just a Spoon and a Bowl

From the kitchen of
Artisan Bread with Steve

Updated 3.24.2020

By
Steve Gamelin

Copyright © 2014 by Steve Gamelin

All rights reserved. No part of this book may be used or reproduced, stored in a retrieval system, or transmitted in an form or by an means—electronics, mechanical, or any other—except for brief quotations in print reviews without prior permission of the author.

Now that I have met the standard legal requirements I would like to give my personal exceptions. I understand this is a cookbook and anyone who purchases this book can, (a) print and share the recipes with their friends, as you do with your other cookbooks (of course, it is my hope they too will start to make no-knead bread and buy my cookbooks) and (b) you may share a recipe or two on your website, etc. as long as you note the source and provide instructions on how your audience can acquire this book.

Thanks – Steve

Table of Contents

"Table of Contents" lists both recipes and bakeware used to shape loaves and rolls, but you can mix and match... the ingredients from one recipe with the bakeware technique from a different recipe. The two components are independent of each other. Any recipe... any bakeware.

Author's Note

The traditional method for making no-knead bread
uses 3 cups flour and was designed to be baked in a Dutch oven.

When I developed no-knead "Turbo" bread
I designed it to be baked in a bread pan
which uses 3-1/2 cups flour
(loaves using 3 cups flour are
too small for a standard bread pan).

Because I wanted the flexibility of using
any recipe with any baking technique...
I converted the majority of my recipes to 3-1/2 cups flour.

After all, you can always use 3-1/2 cups flour
to make a boule in a Dutch oven,
but you can't use 3 cups flour to make a standard loaf.

Quick Note from Steve

Hi... I'm Steve, my YouTube channel is "ArtisanBreadWithSteve" on which I have a selection of educational videos demonstrating no-knead bread recipes and technique. Over the years I have worked with my readers and subscribers listening to their desires and needs... to have high quality, great tasting, fresh from the oven bread that is fast, convenient, hassle-free, and reliable without special equipment or expensive bakeware. In response, I developed no-knead "Turbo" bread (ready to bake in 2-1/2 hours), "hands-free" technique (bread can go straight from mixing bowl to baking vessel without dusting work surface with flour or touching the dough), and "roll-to-coat" (coat dough with flour in mixing bowl... no more sticky dough).

Now, don't get me wrong... I love the "traditional" method of making no-knead bread, but there are times when I need bread in less time and I can have no-knead "Turbo" bread ready for the oven in less than 2-1/2 hours... without touching the dough!

No-knead "Turbo" bread, "hands-free" technique, and "roll-to-coat" are fresh approaches to making no-knead bread that provides you with an option. Try it... you'll love it.

Thanks - Steve

The Two Basic Methods for Making No-Knead Bread

There are two basic methods... traditional and turbo.

"Traditional" No-Knead Method

The traditional no knead method uses long proofing times (8 to 12 hours) to develop flavor and was designed to be baked in a Dutch oven. The purpose of the Dutch oven is to emulate a baker's oven by trapping the moisture from the dough in a "screaming" hot, enclosed environment. This is an excellent method for making artisan quality bread.

Recommended YouTube video: World's Easiest No-Knead Bread (Introducing "Hands-Free" Technique)

No-Knead "Turbo" Method

The no-knead "Turbo Method" uses shorter proofing times (ready to bake in 2-1/2 hours) and was designed to be baked in traditional bakeware (bread pan, etc.). It was designed for those who want to make no-knead bread, but... don't want to wait 8 to 24 hours. Those who want bread machine bread, but... don't want to buy and store a bread machine. It's for those of you who want a fast reliable way to make fresh from the oven bread without the hustle of expensive machines, Dutch ovens, or kneading.

Recommended YouTube video: Ultimate Introduction to No-Knead "Turbo" Bread... ready to bake in 2-1/2 hours

This cookbook uses the "Turbo" method of making no-knead bread.

Advantages of No-Knead "Turbo" Bread, Rolls, & Pizza are...

(1) Shorter time... bread is ready to bake in less than 2-1/2 hours.

(2) No kneading... Mother Nature does the kneading for you.

(3) No yeast proofing... instant yeast doesn't require proofing.

(4) No special equipment (no mixer, no bread machine) the entire process is done in a glass bowl with a spoon and a spatula... and can be baked in a wide variety of baking vessels (standard bread pan, uncovered baker, skillet, preheated Dutch oven, etc.).

(5) Only uses 4 basic ingredients (flour, salt, yeast and water) to which other ingredients can be added to make a variety of specialty breads.

(6) "Hands-free" technique uses the handle end of a plastic spoon to manipulate the dough (like a dough hook) which allows the dough to go

straight from the mixing bowl to the baking vessel (bread pan, etc.) without dusting the work surface with flour or touching the dough.

(7) And "roll-to-coat"... an innovative process that coats the dough ball with flour... in the mixing bowl... no more sticky dough. When the dough comes out of the bowl it will be easy to handle if you wish to divide the dough into portion to make baguettes, rolls, etc.

Some have said, no-knead "Turbo" bread is bread machine bread... without the bread machine. I like to think of it as a way for the average family to have fresh from the oven bread in the convenience of their homes without special equipment or any hassles.

Ingredients

It only takes four ingredients to make bread... flour, salt, yeast and water.

Flour

Flour is the base ingredient of bread and there are four basic types of flour...

(1) Bread flour is designed for yeast bread. It has a higher percentage of gluten which gives artisan bread its airy crumb.

(2) All-purpose flour has less gluten than bread flour. I use all-purpose flour for biscuits, flatbreads, etc. In other words... I use it when I don't want an airy crumb.

(3) Self-rising flour is all-purpose flour with baking soda and baking powder added as leavening agents. It's intended for quick breads... premixed and ready to go. Do not use self-rising flour to make yeast bread. To see the difference between yeast and quick breads you may want to watch Introduction to No-Knead Beer Bread (a.k.a. Artisan Yeast Beer Bread) and Introduction to Quick Beer Bread (a.k.a. Beer Bread Dinner Rolls).

(4) And there are a variety of specialty flours... whole wheat, rye, and a host of others. Each has its unique flavor and characteristics. In some cases, you can substitute specialty flour for bread flour, but you may need to tweak the recipe because most specialty flours have less gluten. I frequently blend specialty flour with bread flour.

Flour is the primary ingredient... if you don't use the correct flour you won't get the desired results.

Note: To know how many cups of flour there are in a specific bag... it's typically on the side in "Nutritional Facts". For example, this bag reads, "Serving Size 1/4 cup... Serving Per Container about 75". In other words... 18.75 (75 times 1/4). That's the technical answer, but in the real world (measuring cup versus weight) a bag of flour will measure differently based on density (sifted versus unsifted), type of flour (wheat is more dense than bread flour), humidity (flour weighs more on humid days), and all the other variables life and nature have to offer. Thus, there is no single correct answer, but for practical purposes... figure a 5 lb bag of bread flour is 17 to 18 cups.

Salt

While it is possible to make bread without salt... you would be disappointed. There are three basics types of salt...

(1) Most baking recipes are designed to use everyday table salt unless specified otherwise. Unless you're experienced, it is probably smartest to use table salt for your baking needs.

(2) Kosher salt is excellent. I use it when I cook, but a tablespoon of kosher salt does not equal a tablespoon of table salt because kosher salt crystals are larger.

(3) And, I use specialty salt as a garnish... for appearance and taste. For example, I use sea salt to garnish pretzels.

Generally speaking, when salt is added as an ingredient and baked it is difficult to taste the difference between table, kosher and sea salt. When salt is added as a garnish and comes in contact with the taste buds... kosher or specialty salt is an excellent choice.

Yeast

Yeast is the "magic" ingredient which transforms flour and water into dough. Traditional no-knead recipes use 1/4 tsp yeast (we want the dough to rise slowly which allows the dough to develop flavor). "Turbo" recipes use 1-1/4 tsp yeast (ready to bake in 2-1/2 hours). There are three basic types of yeast...

(1) The most common is active dry yeast which is traditionally proofed in warm water prior to being added to flour.

(2) Instant dry yeast (a.k.a. "instant yeast", "bread machine yeast", "quick rise", "rapid rise", "fast rising", etc.) which was designed for bread machines and does not need to be proofed in warm water... why worry about proofing yeast if you don't have too.

(3) Some older recipes call for cake yeast (a.k.a. "compressed yeast" or "fresh yeast"), but it's perishable. You can substitute active and instant dry yeast for cake yeast when using older recipes.

Update: While I respect the history of bread making and opinions of others, I do all my own testing. And, when I designed "Turbo" bread I found proofing technique was more important than the amount of yeast. In other words... when I proofed at 78 to 85 degrees F. it didn't make any difference if I use 1-1/4 or 2-1/4 ounces yeast... I got the same results. The reason is... the manufacturing of yeast has significantly improved yeast (more live yeast and better strains) since the 1940's when recipes called for a 2-1/4 ounce packet of yeast. When you bake a lot, you can save a lot by reducing the amount is yeast.

Furthermore, because the quality of dry yeast has improved... I now believe active dry yeast and instant yeast are interchangeable. Active dry yeast is a different stain of yeast (designed to act faster), but for all practical purposes the results is very similar.

Water

Water hydrates the ingredients and activates the yeast. The no-knead method uses a little more water than the typical recipe... and that's a good thing. It makes it easier to combine the wet and dry ingredients, and contributes to its airy crumb.

(1) I use tap water. It's convenient and easy, but sometimes city water has too much chlorine (chlorine kills yeast).

(2) If your dough does not rise during first proofing you may want to use bottled drinking water.

(3) But, do not use distilled water because the minerals have been removed.

Water is a flavor ingredient, if your water doesn't taste good... use bottled drinking water.

Flavor Ingredients

It only takes four ingredients to make bread... flour, salt, yeast and water, to which a variety of flavor ingredients can be added to make specialty breads such as... honey whole wheat, multi-grain white, rosemary, Mediterranean olive, cinnamon raisin, honey oatmeal, and a host of others.

Technique & Tips

The technique discussed in this section is demonstrated on YouTube in Introduction to No-Knead "Turbo" Bread (updated)... ready to bake in 2-1/2 hours (super easy).

Prep

To insure consistency and assist Mother Nature with proofing... it's important to provide yeast with a warm proofing environment. One of the keys to proofing temperature is the temperature of the mixing bowl because it has direct contact with the dough. Thus, use a bowl that is warm to the touch so that the bowl doesn't draw the heat out of the warm water.

Combining Ingredients

Pour water in a 3 to 4 qt glass mixing bowl (use warm water and a warm bowl for "Turbo" and cool for traditional). Add salt, yeast, flavor ingredients, etc... and stir to combine (it will insure the ingredients are evenly distributed). Add flour (flour will resist the water and float). Start by stirring the ingredients with the handle end of a plastic spoon drawing the flour from the sides into the middle of bowl (vigorously mixing will not hydrate the flour faster... but it will raise a lot of dust). Within 30 seconds the flour will hydrate and form a shaggy ball. Then scrape dry flour from side of bowl and tumble dough to combine moist flour with dry flour (about 15 seconds). It takes about one minute to combine wet and dry ingredients.

Cover bowl with plastic wrap, place in a warm draft free location, and proof for 1-1/2 hours.

1st Proofing (bulk fermentation)

The process is called "proofing" because it "proves" the yeast is active.

Bread making is nature at work (yeast is a living organism) and subject to nature. Seasons (summer vs. winter) and weather (heat & humidity) have a direct impact on proofing. In other words, don't worry if your dough varies in size... that's Mother Nature. Just focus on your goal... if the gluten forms (dough develops a stringy nature) and doubles in size... you're good to go.

If your dough does not rise the usual culprits are... outdated yeast or chlorinated water (chlorine kills yeast). Solution, get fresh yeast and/or use bottled drinking water.

If your dough is slow (takes "forever") to rise... your proofing temperature is probably too cool.

Because "Turbo" dough use shorter proofing times (1-12/ hours) it is important to practice sound proofing technique.

The ideal temperature for proofing is 78 to 85 degrees F, but the typically home is 68 to 72 degrees, which is why recipes generally suggest proofing in a "warm draft-free environment". So, you have a choice... wait longer or create a warm proofing environment. My favorites are...

Oven setting: If your oven has a setting for proofing (80 degrees F)... use it.

Direct sunlight: Cover bowl with plastic wrap, place in direct sunlight, and the heat from the Sun will create a favorable proofing environment.

Oven light: If your oven has a light... cover bowl with plastic wrap, place in oven, turn light on, and close the door. The oven light will generate heat and increase the temperature inside the oven by several degrees. The amount of heat will depend on the size of the oven and strength of the bulb. The oven temperature will always start low and climb slowly, but it may go over 90 degrees F. so check periodically until you are familiar with the nature of your oven.

Desk Lamp: Cover bowl with plastic wrap, place under a desk lamp, lower lamp so that it's close to the bowl, and turn lamp on. The plastic wrap over the bowl will create a similar effect to leaving car windows rolled up on a sunny day.

Microwave: Place an 8 to 16 oz cup of water in the microwave and heat on high for 2 minutes. Then move the cup to the back corner, place mixing bowl (dough) in microwave and close the door. The heat and steam from the hot water will create a favorable environment for proofing.

Folding dough proofer: Commercial bakeries have large proofing ovens in which they can control climate and temperature. There are smaller versions available for the public that fold flat.

Tip: To fit bread making into your schedule... you can extend 1st proofing up to 4 hours (or even more), but don't shorten... it important to give Mother Nature time to form the gluten.

Degas, Pull & Stretch

The purpose of degassing, pulling and stretching is to, (a) expel the gases that formed during bulk fermentation, (b) strengthen the dough by realigning and stretching the gluten strands, and (c) stimulate yeast activity for 2nd proofing.

Because no-knead dough is sticky and difficult to handle... I degas, pull & stretch dough by stirring it in the bowl with the handle end of a plastic spoon (like a dough hook). It will reduce the size of the dough ball by 50% making it easier to handle and the process replaces folding and shaping in most cases.

Roll-to-Coat

Before removing the dough from bowl... dust the dough and side of the bowl with flour, then roll-to-coat. The flour will bond to the sticky dough making it easier to handle, but do not roll-to-coat with flour if you're going to garnish or baste.

Garnish & Baste

The purpose of garnishing and basting is to enhance the appearance of the crust, but it isn't necessary. If you decide to garnish and baste there are two techniques... roll-to-coat and skillet method.

Roll-to-Coat Method: Before removing dough from bowl... add ingredients to bowl (on the dough and side of the bowl), then roll to coat. For example, when I garnish honey oatmeal bread... I sprinkle oat in the bowl and on the dough, then roll the dough ball in the oats and they will bond to the sticky dough. This can also be done with seeds, grains, olive oil, egg wash, etc.

Skillet Method: When I want to garnish and/or baste the top of the loaf... I coat the proofing skillet with baste (egg wash, olive oil, vegetable oil, etc.) and sprinkle with the garnish (oats, seeds, grains, etc.). The ingredients will bond with the dough as the dough proofs.

Supporting video: How to Garnish & Baste No-Knead Bread using "Hands-Free" Technique

Divide & Shape

If you're not going to divide the dough... it can go straight from the mixing bowl to the proofing skillet or baking vessel. If you are going to divide and shape the dough... dust the dough and side of the bowl with flour and roll-to-coat, dust work surface with flour, roll the dough ball out of the bowl (excess flour and all) onto the work surface, and divide and shape. I use a plastic bowl scraper to assist in dividing, shaping and carry the dough to the baking vessel. Together they (flour & bowl scraper) make it easier to handle the dough.

2nd Proofing

Place dough in a warm draft-free location and proof for 30 minutes.

Tip: To fit bread making into your schedule... you can extend 2nd proofing times, but you don't want the dough to exceed the size of the baking vessel. If you're using a large baking vessel (Dutch oven, etc.) it's never a problem, but if you're using a bread pan don't allow the dough to exceed the sides of the pan before baking or your loaf will droop over the sides and be less attractive. But, always bake it... it will still be delicious.

Score

The purpose of scoring dough is to provide seams to control where the crust will split during "oven spring", but it isn't necessary to score dough. If you do decide to score your loaf you may want to use a scissors (no-knead dough is very moist and more likely to stretch than slice). Personally, I place the dough in the baking vessel seam side up... the dough will split at the seam during "oven spring" which gives the loaf a nice rustic appearance.

Bake

Baking Time: Bread is done when it reaches an internal temperature of 185 to 220 degrees F. and the crumb (inside of the bread) isn't doughy. Baking times in my recipes are designed to give bread an internal temperature of 200 to 205 degrees F, but ovens vary and you may need to adjust your baking times slightly.

No-Stick Spray: Most bakeware has a non-stick surface, but it is safest to spray your bakeware unless you are fully confident your bread won't stick.

Ovens: Ovens aren't always accurate. I check the temperature of ovens and bakeware. Ovens with a digital readout that displays the temperature as they preheat are typically very accurate, but ovens that say they will be at temperature in a specific number of minutes are not always accurate. My point is... you will get the best results if you learn the character and nature of your oven.

Oven Rack: Generally speaking you want to bake bread and rolls in the middle or lower third of the oven, but it isn't critical. Just keep them away from the upper heating element or they may brown a little too quickly.

Oven Spring: When dough is first put into the oven it will increase in size by as much as a third in a matter of minutes because, (a) gases trapped in the dough will expand, (b) moisture will turn into steam and try to push its way out, and (c) yeast will become highly active converting sugars into gases. The steam and gases work together to create "oven spring". Once the internal temperature of the bread reaches 120 degrees F... the yeast will begin to die and the crust will harden.

Storing Bread & Dough

After allowing bread to cool... it can be wrapped in plastic wrap, or stored in a zip-lock plastic bag, or plastic bread bags (available on the web). If you wish to keep bread for a longer period of time... slice it into portions and freeze them in a zip-lock freezer bag (remove excess air). Do not store bread in the refrigerator. Bread goes stale faster in the refrigerator.

If you wish to save dough... divide it into portions, drizzle each portion with olive oil, place in zip-lock bag, remove excess air, and refrigerate for up to two days or freeze for up to two months. To thaw dough... move dough from freezer to refrigerator the day before (12 or more hours), then place on counter for 30 minutes before use to come to room temperature.

Equipment & Bakeware

Bowl for Mixing: You can use any 3 to 4 qt bowl. I use a 3-1/2 qt glass bowl because, (a) there's ample room for the dough to expand, (b) plastic wrap sticks to glass, and (c) I don't want the rim of my bowl to exceed the width of the plastic wrap.

Measuring Spoons: I'm sure you already have measuring spoons in the kitchen... they will work just fine. If you're going to buy new, I prefer oval versus round because an oval shape will fit into jars and containers more easily.

Measuring Cups: Dry measuring cups are designed to be filled to the top and leveled. Liquid measuring cups have a pour spout and are designed to be filled to the gradations on the side (neither measures weight). It is best to use the appropriate measuring cup.

Note: U.S. and metric measuring cups may be used interchangeably... there is only a slight difference (±3%). More importantly, the ingredients of a recipe measured with a set (U.S. or metric) will have their volumes in the same proportion to one another.

Spoon for Combining Wet and Dry Ingredients: A spoon is an excellent tool for combining wet and dry ingredients. Surprisingly, I found the handle end of a plastic spoon worked best for me because, I didn't have a big clump on the end like some of my other mixing utensils (which makes it easier to stir and manipulate the dough). And when you think about it... mixers don't use a paddle to mix dough, they use a hook which looks a lot like the handle end of my spoon.

Silicon Baking Mat: Silicone baking mats are very useful... I use them as reusable parchment paper (they're environmentally friendly). Silicone baking mats serve two purposes... (a) as a work surface for folding and shaping (they have excellent non-stick properties), and (b) as a baking mat... specifically when the dough is difficult to move after folding and shaping. And I slide a cookie sheet under the mat before baking (it makes it easier to put the mat into and take it out of the oven).

Spatula: I use a spatula to scrape the sides of the bowl to get the last bits of flour incorporated into the dough.

Plastic Bowl Scraper: I use a plastic bowl scraper verses a metal dough scraper because it's the better multi-tasker. I use the bowl scraper to (a) fold, shape, and divide the dough, (b) assist in transporting the dough to the proofing vessel, (c) scrape excess flour off the work surface, (d) scrape excess flour out of the bowl (after all it is a bowl scraper), and (e) scrape any remaining bits in the sink towards the disposal. It's a useful multi-tasker and you can't do all those tasks with a metal cough scraper.

Timer: I'm sure you already have a timer and it will work just fine. If you're thinking about a new one... I prefer digital because they're more accurate.

Proofing Baskets & Vessels: The purpose of a proofing basket or vessel is to pre-shape the dough prior to baking (dough will spread if it isn't contained). Because no-knead dough has a tendency to stick to the lining of proofing baskets... I use common household items as proofing vessels. For example, I use an 8" skillet (with no-stick spray) to pre-shape dough when baking in a Dutch oven. It shapes the dough during proofing, and the handle makes it easy to carry the dough and put it in the hot Dutch oven safely.

You can also proof dough in the baking vessel if it doesn't have to be preheated. For example, standard loaves are typically proof and baked in the bread pan where your bread pan shapes the loaf during proofing and baking. You can use this same principle for shaping and baking rolls and buns.

Baking Vessels: Baking vessels come in a variety of sizes, shapes and materials. You can change the appearance of the loaf by sampling changing the baking vessel.

Plastic Wrap & Proofing Towel: I use plastic wrap for 1st proofing and a lint-free towel for 2nd proofing. Plastic wrap protects dough for longer proofing times and can be used to create a favorable proofing environment (solar effect).

Cooling Rack: The purpose of a cooling rack is to expose the bottom of the loaf during the cooling process.

Bread Bags: I use plastic bread bags to store bread after they have cooled. And they're great for packaging bread as gifts. I also use paper bags as gifts when the loaf is still warm and I don't want to trap the moisture in a plastic bag... it gives a nice natural appearance.

10" Flat Whisk: I use a flat whisk to combine dry ingredients with yogurt... a flat whisk will slice through yogurt forming small clump. If you use a balloon whisk a big lump will form inside the balloon.

Pastry/Pizza Roller: When you watch shows they hand shape and toss pizza dough, but I find it more practical to use a pastry/pizza roller. It is also useful when shaping flatbread and cinnamon rolls.

Impact of Weather on Bread Making

Elevations: Higher elevations have lower air pressure. As a result, yeast creates larger bubbles and the dough rises too fast... before properly developing flavor and texture. Solution, proof in a cool location or refrigerator to slow fermentation. Higher elevations will also cause dehydration, but that usually isn't a problem because no-knead dough has a high moisture content.

Humidity: Low humidity makes ingredients dryer and high humidity adds moisture to ingredients (especially flour). Fortunately bread making is very forgiving, but there are times you will want to make minor adjustments. For example, on cold winter days with low humidity you may want to add 1 to 2 ounces of water if the dough is dryer than normal. For high humidity, I have never found it necessary to reduce the amount of water, because I can always "roll-to-coat" the dough in flour to make it easier to handle.

Temperature: The ideal temperature for proofing dough is 78 to 85 degrees F. Dough takes longer to proof in cooler temperatures (77 degrees and lower) and dough proofs faster in warm temperatures (86 degrees and higher). Thus, when the house is cold I extend the proofing time from 8 to 24 hours using the "traditional" method. And, I use the "oven light method" of proofing to create a warm draft free environment for proofing when using the "Turbo" method. When the house is warm, you can start any time the dough is ready.

Bread

One simple recipe, four ingredients, no kneading, no yeast proofing, no mixer... just a little tweaking and you can create a variety of artisan breads that you would be proud to serve your family and friends.

To further expand your repertoire, these recipes have a dual purpose... ingredients for specific breads and technique (bakeware/methods). The recipes use...

Small bread pan
Bread pan
Long loaf pan
Baguette pan
Skillet
Poor man's Dutch oven
Preheated Dutch oven
Uncovered baker
Preheated uncovered baker
Long covered baker
Mini round baker
Pie pan

My point is... you can use the ingredients from one recipe and the technique (bakeware) from another. The options are endless.

Country White Bread (bread pan)
Country White is the most popular artisan bread. It's simple... it's basic. And, if you're making your first loaf... this is the place to start.

I used a *Chicago Metallic* bread pan (8-1/2" x 4-1/2") to shape this loaf. The bread pan is the #1 baking vessel for bread (most common), but you can use any anything from a preheated Dutch oven (the traditional no-knead method) to an uncovered baker.

YouTube Video in support of recipe: Introduction to No-Knead Turbo Bread (Ready to Bake in 2-1/2 Hours with Just a Spoon and a Bowl)

Country White Bread

Pour warm water in a 3 to 4 qt warm glass mixing bowl (use a warm bowl... you don't want a cold bowl to take the heat out of the warm water).

14 oz warm Water

Add salt and yeast... give a quick stir to combine.

1-1/2 tsp Salt

1-1/4 tsp Instant Yeast

Add flour... stir until dough forms a shaggy ball, scrape dry flour from side of bowl, then tumble dough to combine moist flour with dry flour.

3-1/2 cups Bread Flour

Cover bowl with plastic wrap, place in a warm draft-free location, and proof for 1-1/2 hours.

1-1/2 hours later (bread pan)

When dough has risen and developed its gluten structure... spray the bread pan (8-1/2" x 4-1/2" or 9" x 5") with no-stick cooking spray and set aside.

"Degas, pull and stretch"... stick handle end of a plastic spoon in the dough and stir (dough will form a sticky ball). Then, scrape side of bowl to get remainder of the dough into the sticky dough ball.

Roll dough out of bowl into bread pan.

Place pan in a warm draft-free location, cover with a lint-free towel, and proof for 30 minutes.

Before dough is fully proofed...

Move rack to middle of oven and pre-heat to 400 degrees F.

30 minutes later

When oven has come to temperature... place bread pan in oven and bake for 40 minutes.

40 minutes later

Gently turn loaf out on work surface and place on cooling rack.

Skillet Bread (skillet)
Simple recipe... simple technique... great results, and I garnished the loaf with sesame seed. It's really very simple. I didn't even have to touch the dough.

I used a *Lodge* cast iron 10-1/2" skillet to shape this loaf, but you can use any 8" to 10-1/2" oven safe skillet (make sure the handle is oven safe). A smaller 8" skillet will constrain the dough during oven bounce and force the dough to expand upwards and give you a tall plump boule, while a larger 10-1/2" skillet will allow the dough to expand outwards filling the skillet and give you a broad low profile boule.

YouTube Video in support of recipe: How to Bake No-Knead "Turbo" Bread in a Skillet (ready to bake in 2-1/2 hours)

Skillet Bread

Pour warm water in a 3 to 4 qt warm glass mixing bowl (use a warm bowl... you don't want a cold bowl to take the heat out of the warm water).

14 oz warm Water

Add salt and yeast... give a quick stir to combine.

1-1/2 tsp Salt
1-1/4 tsp Instant Yeast

Add flour... stir until dough forms a shaggy ball, scrape dry flour from side of bowl, then tumble dough to combine moist flour with dry flour.

3-1/2 cups Bread Flour

Cover bowl with plastic wrap, place in a warm draft-free location, and proof for 1-1/2 hours.

1-1/2 hours later (skillet | garnish)

When dough has risen and developed its gluten structure... spray skillet with no-stick cooking spray and set aside.
"Degas, pull and stretch"... stick handle end of a plastic spoon in the dough and stir (dough will form a sticky ball). Then, scrape side of bowl to get remainder of the dough into the sticky dough ball.
Garnish... sprinkle dough and side of bowl with seeds and roll-to-coat.

2 Tbsp Sesame Seeds

"Roll-to-coat"... sprinkle dough ball and side of bowl with flour and roll-to-coat.

2 Tbsp Bread Flour

Place skillet in a warm draft-free location, cover with a lint-free towel, and proof for 30 minutes.

Before dough is fully proofed...

Move rack to middle of oven and pre-heat to 400 degrees F.

30 minutes later

When oven has come to temperature... place skillet in oven and bake for 40 minutes.

40 minutes later

Gently turn loaf out on work surface and place on cooling rack.

Sandwich Bread (small poor man's Dutch oven)
Want a Dutch oven that will shape sandwich bread… no problem… use a "poor man's Dutch oven". You'll get a kick out of this recipe. It's unconventional, it's silly, but who cares because the technique is so good that it has become our standard for making sandwich bread.

I used two *Good Cook* (8" x 4" x 2-1/4") loaf pans to shape this loaf. I liked the size and the handles made it easy to clip the top to the bottom.

Option: Because of the pans smaller size (4" x 8" vs. 4-1/2" x 8-1/2" or 9" x 5") I used 3 cups flour. If you use a larger size pan… use 14 oz water, 3-1/2 cups flour, 1-1/2 tsp salt, and 1-1/4 tsp yeast and bake for 40 minutes.

YouTube Video in support of recipe: How to Bake No-Knead Bread in a Poor Man's Dutch Oven (no mixer… no bread machine)

Sandwich Bread

Pour warm water in a 3 to 4 qt warm glass mixing bowl (use a warm bowl... you don't want a cold bowl to take the heat out of the warm water).

<u>12 oz warm Water</u>

Add salt and yeast... give a quick stir to combine.

<u>1-1/2 tsp Salt</u>
<u>1 tsp Instant Yeast</u>

Add flour... stir until dough forms a shaggy ball, scrape dry flour from side of bowl, then tumble dough to combine moist flour with dry flour.

<u>3 cups Bread Flour</u>

Cover bowl with plastic wrap, place in a warm draft-free location, and proof for 1-1/2 hours.

1-1/2 hours later (small poor man's Dutch oven)

When dough has risen and developed its gluten structure... spray bottom pan with no-stick spray and set aside.

"Degas, pull and stretch"... stick handle end of a plastic spoon in the dough and stir (dough will form a sticky ball). Then, scrape side of bowl to get remainder of the dough into the sticky dough ball.

Roll dough out of bowl into bread pan.

Cover bottom bread pan with top pan and place in a warm draft-free location to proof for 30 minutes.

Before dough is fully proofed...

Move rack to lower third of oven and pre-heat to 400 degrees F.

30 minutes later

When oven has come to temperature... place "poor man's Dutch oven" in the oven and bake for 35 minutes with the top on.

35 minutes later

Take PMDO out of the oven, remove the top, and place pan back in the oven for 3 to 15 minutes to finish the crust.

3 to 15 minutes later

Gently turn loaf out on work surface and place on cooling rack.

American Baguettes (baguette pan)

Baguettes are very popular because of their shape. They're ideally suited for garlic cheese bread, bruschetta, sandwiches, etc.

I used 2 *Matfer* 311141 double loaf French bread pan (18"x 2") because they have a smooth baking surface. Previously I used perforated baguette pans, but I had too much trouble with the dough sticking in the perforations.

YouTube Video in support of recipe: Easy No-Knead "Turbo" Baguettes... ready to bake in 2-1/2 hours

American Baguettes

Pour warm water in a 3 to 4 qt warm glass mixing bowl (use a warm bowl... you don't want a cold bowl to take the heat out of the warm water).

14 oz warm Water

Add salt and yeast... give a quick stir to combine.

1-1/2 tsp Salt

1-1/4 tsp Instant Yeast

Add flour... stir until dough forms a shaggy ball, scrape dry flour from side of bowl, then tumble dough to combine moist flour with dry flour.

3-1/2 cups Bread Flour

Cover bowl with plastic wrap, place in a warm draft-free location, and proof for 1-1/2 hours.

1-1/2 hours later (baguette pan)

When dough has risen and developed its gluten structure... spray baguette pans with no-stick spray and set aside.

"Degas, pull and stretch"... stick handle end of a plastic spoon in the dough and stir (dough will form a sticky ball). Then, scrape side of bowl to get remainder of the dough into the sticky dough ball.

"Roll-to-coat"... sprinkle dough ball and side of bowl with flour and roll-to-coat (dusting dough ball with flour will make it easier to handle and shape the dough).

2 Tbsp Bread Flour

Dust work surface with flour, roll dough (and excess flour) out of bowl onto work surface.

Press lightly to flatten... and divide dough into 3 portions.

Then (one portion at a time) roll dough on work surface in flour to shape and stretch into 14" lengths and place in baguette pan.

Place pans in a warm draft-free location, cover with lint-free towel, and proof for 30 minutes.

Before dough is fully proofed...

Move rack to middle of oven and pre-heat to 450 degrees F.

30 minutes later

When the dough has proofed and oven has come to temperature... place pans in oven and bake for 25 minutes depending on how you like your crust.

25 minutes later

Remove from oven, gently turn baguettes out on work surface, and place on cooling rack.

Beer Bread (mini round baker | half loaves)

The purpose of this recipe is to introduce those of you who make beer bread to the no-knead method of making dough and introduce those of you who make no-knead bread to beer bread. One simple recipe with hundreds of options... change the wet ingredient—the beer—from a lager, to an amber, or a hefeweizen you can have a new and uniquely flavored bread. It's fun to experiment with beer bread... the beer isle is full of ideas.

There are two basic types of beer bread... yeast and quick. Yeast beer bread uses yeast as a leavening agent. The yeast gives the loaf an airy crumb and artisan quality. Quick beer bread uses self-rising flour which has baking soda and baking powder as leavening agents. Quick beer bread is—as the name implies—very quick and easy, but don't let that fool you. It makes delicious rolls. To see the difference between yeast and quick beer bread you may want to watch Introduction to No-Knead Beer Bread (a.k.a. Artisan Yeast Beer Bread) and Introduction to Quick Beer Bread (a.k.a. Beer Bread Dinner Rolls).

I use 2 *Lodge* cast iron mini round bakers (6") to shape these loaves... I love them. And half loaves are convenient... you can put one at each end to the table.

Beer Bread

Pour room temperature beer in a 3 to 4 qt warm glass mixing bowl (use a warm bowl... you don't want a cold bowl to take the warmth out of the beer).

14 oz room temperature Beer

Add salt and yeast... give a quick stir to combine.

1-1/2 tsp Salt

1-1/4 tsp Instant Yeast

Add flour... stir until dough forms a shaggy ball, scrape dry flour from side of bowl, then tumble dough to combine moist flour with dry flour.

3-1/2 cups Bread Flour

Cover bowl with plastic wrap, place in a warm draft-free location, and proof for 1-1/2 hours.

1-1/2 hours later (mini round baker | half loaves)

When dough has risen and developed its gluten structure... spray mini round bakers with no-stick spray and set aside.

"Degas, pull and stretch"... stick handle end of a plastic spoon in the dough and stir (dough will form a sticky ball). Then, scrape side of bowl to get remainder of the dough into the sticky dough ball.

"Roll-to-coat"... sprinkle dough ball and side of bowl with flour and roll-to-coat (dusting dough ball with flour will make it easier to handle and shape the dough).

2 Tbsp Bread Flour

Dust work surface with flour, roll dough (and excess flour) out of bowl onto work surface.

Divide dough into 2 portions.

Then (one portion at a time) roll dough on work surface, form a ball, and place in baker.

Place bakers in a warm draft-free location, cover with a lint-free towel, and proof for 30 minutes.

Before dough is fully proofed...

Move rack to middle of oven and pre-heat to 400 degrees F.

30 minutes later

When oven has come to temperature... place bakers in oven and bake for 35 minutes.

35 minutes later

Gently turn loaves out on work surface and place on cooling rack.

Cheddar Cheese Bread (preheated Dutch oven)
Fresh from the oven bread is special... add cheese and you have a winner. Something your friends and guests will love. This is a remarkably simple recipe that everyone will enjoy.

This recipe uses the traditional no-knead method (preheated Dutch oven), baking time and temperature. And, I used a 2.6 qt *Emile Henry* flame top ceramic Dutch oven (8") to shape this loaf because it gives me a nice plump boule, but you can use any 2-1/2 qt to 5 qt Dutch oven.

Cheddar Cheese Bread

Pour warm water in a 3 to 4 qt warm glass mixing bowl (use a warm bowl... you don't want a cold bowl to take the heat out of the warm water).

16 oz warm Water

Add salt and yeast... give a quick stir to combine.

1-1/2 tsp Salt

1-1/4 tsp Instant Yeast

Add flour... then cheese (if cheese is added before flour it will be harder to combine)... stir until dough forms a shaggy ball, scrape dry flour from side of bowl, then tumble dough to combine moist flour with dry flour.

3-1/2 cups Bread Flour

1 cup coarse shredded Cheddar Cheese

Cover bowl with plastic wrap, place in a warm draft-free location, and proof for 1-1/2 hours.

1-1/2 hours later (preheated Dutch oven)

When dough has risen and developed its gluten structure... spray an 8" proofing skillet with no-stick cooking spray and set aside.

"Degas, pull and stretch"... stick handle end of a plastic spoon in the dough and stir (dough will form a sticky ball). Then, scrape side of bowl to get remainder of the dough into the sticky dough ball.

"Roll-to-coat"... sprinkle dough ball and side of bowl with flour and roll-to-coat.

2 Tbsp Bread Flour

Roll dough out of bowl into proofing skillet.

Place skillet in a warm draft-free location, cover with a lint-free towel, and proof for 30 minutes.

Before dough is fully proofed...

Move rack to lower third of the oven, place Dutch oven in oven and pre-heat to 450 degrees F.

30 minutes later

When oven has come to temperature... remove Dutch oven from oven, transfer dough from proofing skillet to Dutch oven, shake to center, place back in oven and bake for 30 minutes with the top on.

30 minutes later

Take it out of the oven, remove top, and place back in the oven for 3 to 15 minutes to finish the crust... depending on how rustic (hard) you like your crust.

3 to 15 minutes later

Gently turn loaf out on work surface and place on cooling rack.

Multigrain Country White Bread (bread pan)

This is one of my most popular loaves. My first multigrain loaves used 2 cups bread flour and 1 cup wheat flour. One time I forgot the wheat flour and used 3 cups bread flour. Surprise, surprise, surprise... the multigrain country white became one of my most popular breads. I had assumed those who liked grains... liked wheat breads, but there appears to be a significant segment of our society who likes multigrain bread without the wheat bread taste. Wheat is one of those things you either like or don't like, but it doesn't mean you don't like multigrain bread.

I use a *Lodge* L4LP3 cast iron bread pan (8-1/4" x 4-1/2" x 2-1/2") to shape this loaf, but you can use any bread pan without changing baking time or temperature.

Multigrain Country White Bread

Pour warm water in a 3 to 4 qt warm glass mixing bowl (use a warm bowl... you don't want a cold bowl to take the heat out of the warm water).

<u>16 oz warm Water</u>

Add salt, yeast and seeds... give a quick stir to combine.

<u>1-1/2 tsp Salt</u>
<u>1-1/4 tsp Instant Yeast</u>
<u>1 Tbsp Sesame Seeds</u>
<u>1 Tbsp Flax Seeds</u>

Add flour... then oats (if oats are added before flour they will absorb the water and it will be harder to combine)... stir until dough forms a shaggy ball, scrape dry flour from side of bowl, then tumble dough to combine moist flour with dry flour.

<u>3-1/2 cups Bread Flour</u>
<u>1/2 cup Old Fashioned Quaker Oats</u>

Cover bowl with plastic wrap, place in a warm draft-free location, and proof for 1-1/2 hours.

1-1/2 hours later (bread pan | garnish)

When dough has risen and developed its gluten structure... spray the bread pan (8-1/2" x 4-1/2" or 9" x 5") with no-stick cooking spray and set aside.

"Degas, pull and stretch"... stick handle end of a plastic spoon in the dough and stir (dough will form a sticky ball). Then, scrape side of bowl to get remainder of the dough into the sticky dough ball.

Garnish... sprinkle dough ball and side of bowl with oats and roll-to-coat.

<u>1/4 cup Old Fashioned Quaker Oats</u>

"Roll-to-coat"... sprinkle dough ball and side of bowl with flour and roll-to-coat.

<u>2 Tbsp Bread Flour</u>

Roll dough out of bowl into bread pan.

Place pan in a warm draft-free location, cover with a lint-free towel, and proof for 30 minutes.

Before dough is fully proofed...

Move rack to middle of oven and pre-heat to 400 degrees F.

30 minutes later

When oven has come to temperature... place bread pan in oven and bake for 40 minutes.

40 minutes later

Gently turn loaf out on work surface and place on cooling rack.

Italian Sesame Sandwich Bread (poor man's Dutch oven)
For the Italian sesame sandwich bread I used a "poor-man's-Dutch oven". It's the best of both worlds... the shape of sandwich bread using the principles of a Dutch oven. I used two 8-1/2" x 4-1/2" OXO bread pans, but 9" x 5" pans are perfectly acceptable.

Optional:
Add sesame and flax seed to dough... you can create an interesting appearance, texture and flavor by adding 1 Tbsp (each) sesame and flax seeds to the dough.

YouTube Video in support of recipe: No-Knead Bread 101 (Includes demonstration of Sesame Seed Bread... Italian, Muffuletta, & Sandwich)

Italian Sesame Sandwich Bread

Pour warm water in a 3 to 4 qt warm glass mixing bowl (use a warm bowl... you don't want a cold bowl to take the heat out of the warm water).

14 oz warm Water

Add salt, yeast and olive oil... give a quick stir to combine.

1-1/2 tsp Salt
1-1/4 tsp Instant Yeast
1 Tbsp Extra Virgin Olive Oil
1 Tbsp Sesame Seeds (optional)

Add flour... stir until dough forms a shaggy ball, scrape dry flour from side of bowl, then tumble dough to combine moist flour with dry flour.

3-1/2 cups Bread Flour

Cover bowl with plastic wrap, place in a warm draft-free location, and proof for 1-1/2 hours.

1-1/2 hours later (poor man's Dutch oven | garnish)

When dough has risen and developed its gluten structure... spray bottom bread pan (8-1/2" x 4-1/2" or 9" x 5") with no-stick cooking spray and set aside.
"Degas, pull and stretch"... stick handle end of a plastic spoon in the dough and stir (dough will form a sticky ball). Then, scrape side of bowl to get remainder of the dough into the sticky dough ball.
Garnish... sprinkle dough ball and side of bowl with sesame seeds and roll-to-coat.

2 Tbsp Sesame Seeds

"Roll-to-coat"... sprinkle dough ball and side of bowl with flour and roll-to-coat.

2 Tbsp Bread Flour

Roll dough out of bowl into bread pan.
Cover bottom bread pan with top pan and place in a warm draft-free location to proof for 30 minutes.

Before dough is fully proofed...

Move rack to lower third of oven and pre-heat to 400 degrees F.

30 minutes later

When oven has come to temperature... place "poor man's Dutch oven" in oven and bake for 40 minutes with the top on.

40 minutes later

Take PMDO out of the oven, remove the top, and place pan back in the oven for 3 to 15 minutes to finish the crust.

3 to 15 minutes later

Gently turn loaf out on work surface and place on cooling rack.

Italian Sesame Boule (preheated Dutch oven)
This recipe uses "Turbo" dough with the traditional no-knead baking method (preheated Dutch oven), baking time and temperature. I use a 3 qt *Lodge* enameled cast iron Dutch oven (9-1/2" x 3-1/8") to shape this loaf because it gives the loaf a nice shape, but you can use any 3 to 5 qt Dutch oven.

Optional:
Add sesame and flax seed to dough... you can create an interesting appearance, texture and flavor by adding 1 Tbsp (each) sesame and flax seeds to the dough.

YouTube Video in support of recipe: No-Knead Bread 101 (Includes demonstration of Sesame Seed Bread... Italian, Muffuletta, & Sandwich)

Italian Sesame Boule

Pour warm water in a 3 to 4 qt warm glass mixing bowl (use a warm bowl... you don't want a cold bowl to take the heat out of the warm water).

14 oz warm Water

Add salt, yeast, and olive oil... give a quick stir to combine.

1-1/2 tsp Salt
1-1/4 tsp Instant Yeast
1 Tbsp extra-virgin Olive Oil
1 Tbsp Sesame Seeds (optional)
1 Tbsp Flax Seeds (optional)

Add flour... stir until dough forms a shaggy ball, scrape dry flour from side of bowl, then tumble dough to combine moist flour with dry flour.

3-1/2 cups Bread Flour

Cover bowl with plastic wrap, place in a warm draft-free location, and proof for 1-1/2 hours.

1-1/2 hours later (preheated Dutch oven | garnish)

When dough has risen and developed its gluten structure... spray an 8" proofing skillet with no-stick cooking spray and set aside.

"Degas, pull and stretch"... stick handle end of a plastic spoon in the dough and stir (dough will form a sticky ball). Then, scrape side of bowl to get remainder of the dough into the sticky dough ball.

Garnish... sprinkle dough and side of bowl with sesame seeds and roll-to-coat.

2 Tbsp Sesame Seeds

"Roll-to-coat"... sprinkle dough ball and side of bowl with flour and roll-to-coat.

2 Tbsp Bread Flour

Roll dough out of bowl into proofing skillet.

Place skillet in a warm draft-free location, cover with a lint-free towel, and proof for 30 minutes.

Before dough is fully proofed...

Move rack to lower third of the oven, place Dutch oven in oven and pre-heat to 450 degrees F.

30 minutes later

When oven has come to temperature... remove Dutch oven from oven, transfer dough from proofing skillet to Dutch oven, shake to center, place back in oven and bake for 30 minutes with the top on.

30 minutes later

Remove top and bake for an additional 3 to 15 minutes with the top off to finish the crust.

3 to 15 minutes later

Gently turn loaf out on work surface and place on cooling rack.

Muffuletta - Sicilian Sesame Bread (9" pie pan)

"Muffuletta" (moo-foo-le-th) is both a sandwich and the low profile Sicilian sesame bread use to make the sandwich. A traditional style muffuletta sandwich consists of a muffuletta loaf split horizontally, drizzled with olive oil, covered with layers of thinly sliced meat and cheese, and dressed with olive salad.

YouTube Video in support of recipe: No-Knead Bread 101 (Includes demonstration of Sesame Seed Bread... Italian, Muffuletta, & Sandwich)

Muffuletta - Sicilian Sesame Bread

Pour warm water in a 2-1/2 to 3-1/2 qt warm glass mixing bowl (use a warm bowl... you don't want a cold bowl to take the heat out of the warm water).

8 oz warm Water

Add salt, yeast, and olive oil... give a quick stir to combine.

1 tsp Salt

1 tsp Instant Yeast

2 tsp extra-virgin Olive Oil

Add flour... stir until dough forms a shaggy ball, scrape dry flour from side of bowl, then tumble dough to combine moist flour with dry flour.

2 cups Bread Flour

Place bowl in a warm draft-free location, cover with a lint-free towel (or plastic wrap) and proof for 1-1/2 hours.

1-1/2 hours later (9" pie pan | garnish)

When dough has risen and developed its gluten structure... spray 9" pie pan with no-stick cooking spray (or drizzle with olive oil) and set aside.

"Degas, pull and stretch"... stick handle end of a plastic spoon in the dough and stir (dough will form a sticky ball). Then, scrape side of bowl to get remainder of the dough into the sticky dough ball.

Garnish... sprinkle dough and side of bowl with seeds and roll-to-coat.

2 Tbsp Sesame Seeds

"Roll-to-coat"... sprinkle dough ball and side of bowl with flour and roll-to-coat.

1 Tbsp Bread Flour

Roll dough out of bowl into pie plate and shape into a 9" flat disc. If the dough is springy and difficult to shape... cover with a lint-free towel, rest for 10 minutes (resting dough makes it easier to shape dough), and finish shaping.

Place pan in a warm draft-free location, cover with a lint-free towel, and proof for 30 minutes.

Before dough is fully proofed...

Move rack to middle of oven and pre-heat to 400 degrees F.

30 minutes later

When oven has come to temperature... place pan in oven and bake for 30 minutes.

30 minutes later

Gently turn loaf out on work surface and place on cooling rack.

Honey Oatmeal Bread (uncovered baker)

Fresh from the oven bread with the wholesome goodness of oats and the sweetness of honey... what's not to like? This loaf is as delicious to eat as it is pleasing to the eye and the garnish is very easy to apply giving the loaf a special appearance.

I used a 2 qt *Threshold* stoneware oval baker (10" x 6-3/4" x 2-1/2") to shape the loaf, but any oven-proof dish will work. I like casserole dishes with rounded bottoms... they give loaves a nice shape.

Honey Oatmeal Bread

Pour warm water in a 3 to 4 qt warm glass mixing bowl (use a warm bowl... you don't want a cold bowl to take the heat out of the warm water).

16 oz warm Water

Add salt, yeast, olive oil and honey... give a quick stir to combine.

1-1/2 tsp Salt
1-1/4 tsp Instant Yeast
1 Tbsp extra-virgin Olive Oil
1 Tbsp Honey

Add flour... then oats (if oats are added before flour they will absorb the water and it will be harder to combine)... stir until dough forms a shaggy ball, scrape dry flour from side of bowl, then tumble dough to combine moist flour with dry flour.

3-1/2 cups Bread Flour
1 cup Old Fashioned Quaker Oats

Cover bowl with plastic wrap, place in a warm draft-free location, and proof for 1-1/2 hours.

1-1/2 hours later (uncovered baker | garnish)

When dough has risen and developed its gluten structure... spray baker with no-stick cooking spray and set aside.

"Degas, pull and stretch"... stick handle end of a plastic spoon in the dough and stir (dough will form a sticky ball). Then, scrape side of bowl to get remainder of the dough into the sticky dough ball.

Garnish... sprinkle dough ball and side of bowl with oats and roll-to-coat.

1/4 cup Old Fashioned Quaker Oats

"Roll-to-coat"... sprinkle dough ball and side of bowl with flour and roll-to-coat.

2 Tbsp Bread Flour

Roll dough out of bowl into baker.

Place baker in a warm draft-free location, cover with a lint-free towel, and proof for 30 minutes.

Before dough is fully proofed...

Move rack to middle of oven and pre-heat to 400 degrees F.

30 minutes later

When oven has come to temperature... place baker in oven and bake for 40 minutes.

40 minutes later

Gently turn loaf out on work surface and place on cooling rack.

Honey Whole Wheat Bread (preheated Dutch oven)

This whole wheat recipe balances the nutrition and nutty taste of whole wheat with the crumb of a Country White in a hearty, moist loaf with a touch of honey for sweetness.

Because whole wheat flour has less gluten... 100% whole wheat loaves can be a little too heavy and dense for some tastes. Personally, I like to balance the nutritional value of whole wheat with the crumb and texture of bread flour by using a 50/50 blend. And I used a total of 4 cups flour to create the size loaf I desired.

This recipe uses the traditional no-knead method (preheated Dutch oven), baking time and temperature. And, I use a 3 qt *Lodge* enameled cast iron Dutch oven (9-1/2" x 3-1/8") to shape this loaf because it gives the loaf a nice shape, but you can use any 2-1/2 qt to 5 qt Dutch oven.

Honey Whole Wheat Bread

Pour warm water in a 3 to 4 qt warm glass mixing bowl (use a warm bowl... you don't want a cold bowl to take the heat out of the warm water).

16 oz warm Water

Add salt, yeast, olive oil and honey... give a quick stir to combine.

1-1/2 tsp Salt
1-1/4 tsp Instant Yeast
1 Tbsp extra-virgin Olive Oil
1 Tbsp Honey

Add flour... stir until dough forms a shaggy ball, scrape dry flour from side of bowl, then tumble dough to combine moist flour with dry flour.

2 cups Bread Flour
1-1/2 cups Whole Wheat Flour

Cover bowl with plastic wrap, place in a warm draft-free location, and proof for 1-1/2 hours.

1-1/2 hours later (preheated Dutch oven)

When dough has risen and developed its gluten structure... spray an 8" proofing skillet with no-stick cooking spray and set aside.

"Degas, pull and stretch"... stick handle end of a plastic spoon in the dough and stir (dough will form a sticky ball). Then, scrape side of bowl to get remainder of the dough into the sticky dough ball.

Roll dough out of bowl into proofing skillet.

Place skillet in a warm draft-free location, cover with a lint-free towel, and proof for 30 minutes.

Before dough is fully proofed...

Move rack to lower third of the oven, place Dutch oven in oven and pre-heat to 450 degrees F.

30 minutes later

When oven has come to temperature... remove Dutch oven from oven, transfer dough from proofing skillet to Dutch oven, shake to center, place back in oven and bake for 30 minutes with the top on.

30 minutes later

Take it out of the oven, remove top, and place back in the oven for 3 to 15 minutes to finish the crust... depending on how rustic (hard) you like your crust.

3 to 15 minutes later

Gently turn loaf out on work surface and place on cooling rack.

Harvest 8 Grain Whole Wheat Bread (long covered baker)

This Harvest 8 Grain Wheat Bread has a more robust and complex flavor than the multigrain country white and wheat breads. I experimented with and tested a number of my own multigrain mixtures before I discovered King Arthur's Harvest Grains Blend and (as they state on their website) the whole oat berries, millet, rye flakes and wheat flakes enhance texture while the flax, poppy, sesame, and sunflower seeds add crunch and great, nutty flavor. Wow, the flavor is great... and it's a lot easier and... more practical... to purchase a blend of seeds. You should experiment with blends available in your community.

I use a *Sassafras* superstone oblong covered baker (13-1/2" x 4-1/2" x 2-1/2") to shape this loaf. No special reason... just a good change of pace.

Harvest 8 Grain Whole Wheat Bread

Pour warm water in a 3 to 4 qt warm glass mixing bowl (use a warm bowl... you don't want a cold bowl to take the heat out of the warm water).

16 oz warm Water

Add salt, yeast, grains and olive oil... give a quick stir to combine.

1-1/2 tsp Salt
1-1/4 tsp Instant Yeast
2/3 cup King Arthur Harvest Grains Blend
1 Tbsp extra-virgin Olive Oil

Add flour... stir until dough forms a shaggy ball, scrape dry flour from side of bowl, then tumble dough to combine moist flour with dry flour.

2 cups Bread Flour
1-1/2 cups Whole Wheat Flour

Cover bowl with plastic wrap, place in a warm draft-free location, and proof for 1-1/2 hours.

1-1/2 hours later (long covered baker)

When dough has risen and developed its gluten structure... spray bottom of baker with no-stick spray and set aside.

"Degas, pull and stretch"... stick handle end of a plastic spoon in the dough and stir (dough will form a sticky ball). Then, scrape side of bowl to get remainder of the dough into the sticky dough ball.

"Roll-to-coat"... sprinkle dough ball and side of bowl with flour and roll-to-coat (dusting dough ball with flour will make it easier to handle and shape the dough for the baker).

2 Tbsp Bread Flour

Dust work surface with flour, roll dough (and excess flour) out of bowl onto work surface, roll dough on work surface in flour to shape, and place in baker. Cover with lid, place in a warm draft-free location, and proof for 30 minutes.

Before dough is fully proofed...

Move rack to lower third of the oven and pre-heat to 400 degrees F (baker does not have to be preheated).

30 minutes later

When oven has come to temperature... place baker in oven and bake for 40 minutes with the top on.

40 minutes later

Take it out of the oven, remove top, and place back in the oven for 3 to 15 minutes to finish the crust... depending on how rustic (hard) you like your crust.

3 to 15 minutes later

Gently turn loaf out on work surface and place on cooling rack.

Flax Seed 8 Grain Bread (bread pan)
This loaf combines the nutrition of milled flax seed (high in fiber and omega-3 fatty acids plus lignans) with whole oat berries, millet, rye flakes, wheat flakes, poppy seeds, sesame seeds, and sunflower seeds (King Arthur's Harvest Blend). The flavor is great.

I used a *Chicago Metallic* bread pan (8-1/2" x 4-1/2") to shape this loaf... the bread pan is the #1 baking vessel for bread (most common), but you can use any anything from a preheated Dutch oven (the traditional no-knead method) to an uncovered baker.

Flax Seed 8 Grain Bread

Pour warm water in a 3 to 4 qt warm glass mixing bowl (use a warm bowl... you don't want a cold bowl to take the heat out of the warm water).

16 oz warm Water

Add salt, yeast, grains, olive oil and honey... give a quick stir to combine.

1-1/2 tsp Salt
1-1/4 tsp Instant Yeast
2/3 cup King Arthur Harvest Grains Blend
1 Tbsp Flax Seeds
1 Tbsp extra-virgin Olive Oil
1 Tbsp Honey

Add flour... stir until dough forms a shaggy ball, scrape dry flour from side of bowl, then tumble dough to combine moist flour with dry flour.

2 cups Bread Flour
1-1/2 cups Whole Wheat Flour
1/2 cup Milled Flax Seed

Cover bowl with plastic wrap, place in a warm draft-free location, and proof for 1-1/2 hours.

1-1/2 hours later (bread pan | baste)

When dough has risen and developed its gluten structure... spray the bread pan (8-1/2" x 4-1/2" or 9" x 5") with no-stick cooking spray and set aside.

"Degas, pull and stretch"... stick handle end of a plastic spoon in the dough and stir (dough will form a sticky ball). Then, scrape side of bowl to get remainder of the dough into the sticky dough ball.

Baste... drizzle dough and side of bowl with olive oil and roll dough in oil to coat.

1 Tbsp Olive Oil

Roll dough out of bowl into bread pan.

Place pan in a warm draft-free location, cover with a lint-free towel, and proof for 30 minutes.

Before dough is fully proofed...

Move rack to middle of oven and pre-heat to 400 degrees F.

30 minutes later

When oven has come to temperature... place bread pan in oven and bake for 40 minutes.

40 minutes later

Gently turn loaf out on work surface and place on cooling rack.

Rosemary Appetizer Loaves (cast iron mini round baker | 3 loaves)
I was so thrilled with the appetizer loaves at *Macaroni Grill* that I decided to make my own and developed a rosemary demi loaf recipe that required kneading. Then my wife found a no-knead ciabatta bread recipe in the local newspaper... I was converted. I experimented with no-knead recipes and converted my old rosemary demi loaf recipe to the no-knead method. That was the beginning and I haven't looked back.

I use 3 *Lodge* cast iron mini round bakers (6") to shape these loaves... the cast iron bakers make the loaves look special.

Rosemary Appetizer Bread

Pour warm water in a 3 to 4 qt warm glass mixing bowl (use a warm bowl... you don't want a cold bowl to take the heat out of the warm water).

14 oz warm Water

Add salt, yeast, rosemary and olive oil... give a quick stir to combine.

1-1/2 tsp Salt
1-1/4 tsp Instant Yeast
1 Tbsp dried Rosemary
1 Tbsp extra-virgin Olive Oil

Add flour... stir until dough forms a shaggy ball, scrape dry flour from side of bowl, then tumble dough to combine moist flour with dry flour.

3-1/2 cups Bread Flour

Cover bowl with plastic wrap, place in a warm draft-free location, and proof for 1-1/2 hours.

1-1/2 hours later (cast iron mini round baker | 3 loaves)

When dough has risen and developed its gluten structure... spray 3 mini round bakers with no-stick spray and set aside.

"Degas, pull and stretch"... stick handle end of a plastic spoon in the dough and stir (dough will form a sticky ball). Then, scrape side of bowl to get remainder of the dough into the sticky dough ball.

"Roll-to-coat"... sprinkle dough ball and side of bowl with flour and roll-to-coat (dusting dough ball with flour will make it easier to handle and shape the dough for the baker).

2 Tbsp Bread Flour

Dust work surface with flour, roll dough (and excess flour) out of bowl onto work surface.

Divide dough into 3 portions.

Then (one portion at a time) roll dough on work surface, form a ball, and place in baker.

Place bakers in a warm draft-free location, cover with a lint-free towel, and proof for 30 minutes.

Before dough is fully proofed...

Move rack to middle of oven and pre-heat to 450 degrees F.

30 minutes later

When oven has come to temperature... place bakers in oven and bake for 25 minutes.

25 minutes later

Gently turn loaves out on work surface and place on cooling rack.

Deli Rye Bread (bread pan)

This is a rustic rye bread, with a mild rye flavor and a generous amount of caraway seeds that would be the perfect complement to a pastrami sandwich.

I use a *USA Pan* heavy gage aluminized steel bread pan (8-1/2" x 4-1/2") to shape this loaf because I like to use rye bread for sandwiches, but you can use any anything from a preheated Dutch oven (the traditional no-knead method) to an uncovered baker.

Deli Rye Bread

Pour warm water in a 3 to 4 qt warm glass mixing bowl (use a warm bowl... you don't want a cold bowl to take the heat out of the warm water).

14 oz warm Water

Add salt, yeast, sugar, seeds and olive oil... give a quick stir to combine.

1-1/2 tsp Salt
1-1/4 tsp Instant Yeast
1 Tbsp Sugar
2 Tbsp Caraway Seeds
1 Tbsp extra-virgin Olive Oil

Add flour... stir until dough forms a shaggy ball, scrape dry flour from side of bowl, then tumble dough to combine moist flour with dry flour.

2-1/2 cups Bread Flour
1 cup Rye Flour

Cover bowl with plastic wrap, place in a warm draft-free location, and proof for 1-1/2 hours.

1-1/2 hours later (bread pan)

When dough has risen and developed its gluten structure... spray the bread pan (8-1/2" x 4-1/2" or 9" x 5") with no-stick cooking spray and set aside.

"Degas, pull and stretch"... stick handle end of a plastic spoon in the dough and stir (dough will form a sticky ball). Then, scrape side of bowl to get remainder of the dough into the sticky dough ball.

"Roll-to-coat"... sprinkle dough ball and side of bowl with flour and roll-to-coat.

2 Tbsp Bread Flour

Roll dough out of bowl into bread pan.

Place pan in a warm draft-free location, cover with a lint-free towel, and proof for 30 minutes.

Before dough is fully proofed...

Move rack to middle of oven and pre-heat to 400 degrees F.

30 minutes later

When oven has come to temperature... place bread pan in oven and bake for 40 minutes.

40 minutes later

Gently turn loaf out on work surface and place on cooling rack.

Polenta Bread (preheated uncovered baker)

The term "polenta" is of Italian origin, but polenta (corn grits) is a Native American grain that was not cultivated in Europe until the early 1500's (after Columbus). Coarse ground grits (polenta) adds texture and a depth of flavor which makes very special bread.

I used an *Emerson Creek Pottery* bread baking bowl (2-3/4" x 8") to shape this loaf. According to King Arthur Flour, "For best results, treat your stoneware pan with care. Oil your stoneware pan with neutral-flavored vegetable oil before each use; a nice patina will develop over time. For additional prevention of sticking, sprinkle a thin layer of cornmeal or semolina into the bottom of the oiled pan." And I agree with their suggestions, but I still had a problem with dough sticking. I found it best to preheat the bowl and spray it with no-stick spray until it was seasoned. That is why I am using the bread baking bowl as the example for "preheated uncovered baker".

Polenta Bread

Pour warm water in a 3 to 4 qt warm glass mixing bowl (use a warm bowl... you don't want a cold bowl to take the heat out of the warm water).

    14 oz warm Water

Add salt, yeast, seeds and olive oil... give a quick stir to combine.

    1-1/2 tsp Salt
    1-1/4 tsp Instant Yeast
    1 Tbsp Sesame Seeds
    1 Tbsp Flax Seeds
    1 Tbsp Olive Oil

Add flour... then polenta... stir until dough forms a shaggy ball, scrape dry flour from side of bowl, then tumble dough to combine moist flour with dry flour.

    3-1/2 cups Bread Flour
    1/3 cup Bob's Red Mill Corn Grits (a.k.a. Polenta)

Cover bowl with plastic wrap, place in a warm draft-free location, and proof for 1-1/2 hours.

1-1/2 hours later (preheated uncovered baker | garnish & baste)

When dough has risen and developed its gluten structure... spray an 8" proofing skillet with no-stick cooking spray and set aside.

"Degas, pull and stretch"... stick handle end of a plastic spoon in the dough and stir (dough will form a sticky ball). Then, scrape side of bowl to get remainder of the dough into the sticky dough ball.

Garnish (optional)... sprinkle dough ball and side of bowl with polenta... roll-to-coat.

    2 Tbsp Bob's Red Mill Corn Grits (a.k.a. Polenta)

Baste... drizzle dough and side of bowl with olive oil... roll dough in oil to coat.

    1 Tbsp Olive Oil

Roll dough out of bowl into proofing skillet.

Place skillet in a warm draft-free location, cover with a lint-free towel, and proof for 30 minutes.

Before dough is fully proofed...

Move rack to middle of oven, place baker in oven and pre-heat to 400 degrees F.

30 minutes later

When oven has come to temperature... remove baker from oven, transfer dough from proofing skillet to baker, shake to center, place baker back in oven and bake for 40 to 50 minutes (polenta bread typically has a more rustic crust).

40 to 50 minutes later

Gently turn loaf out on work surface and place on cooling rack.

Mediterranean Olive Bread (long loaf pan | half loaves)

If you like Mediterranean flavors you'll love this bread. It's unique... it's different... it's perfect for that special occasion. If a restaurant served you this loaf as their signature bread... you'd be talking about it for years and it's surprisingly easy it is to make.

I like Mediterranean olive loaves to be long and narrow so I divided the dough in half and used 2 *Wilton* long loaf pans (12" x 4-1/2" x 3-1/8") to shape them. Then we sliced it and served it as an appetizer with cream cheese, pimento cheese spread, deli meat, provolone, etc.

Mediterranean Olive Bread

Prepare flavor ingredients... zest lemon, slice green olives in half, slice kalamata olives in thirds, and set aside.

Zest of 1 Lemon
2-1/4 oz (1 can) sliced Black Olives
1 can stuffed Green Olives (use black olive can to measure)
1 can Pitted Kalamata Olives (use black olive can to measure)

Pour warm water in a 3 to 4 qt warm glass mixing bowl (use a warm bowl... you don't want a cold bowl to take the heat out of the warm water).

16 oz warm Water

Add salt, yeast, thyme, and olive oil... give a quick stir to combine.

1-1/2 tsp Salt
1-1/4 tsp Instant Yeast
1 heaping tsp dried Thyme
1 Tbsp extra-virgin Olive Oil

Add flour... then flavor ingredients. Stir until dough forms a shaggy ball, scrape dry flour from side of bowl, then tumble dough to combine moist flour with dry flour.

4 cups Bread Flour

Cover bowl with plastic wrap, place in a warm draft-free location, and proof for 1-1/2 hours.

1-1/2 hours later (long loaf pan | half loaves)

When dough has risen and developed its gluten structure... spray 2 long bread pans (12" x 4-1/2" x 3-1/8") with no-stick cooking spray and set aside.

"Degas, pull and stretch"... stick handle end of a plastic spoon in the dough and stir (dough will form a sticky ball). Then, scrape side of bowl to get remainder of the dough into the sticky dough ball.

"Roll-to-coat"... sprinkle dough ball and side of bowl with flour and roll-to-coat.

2 Tbsp Bread Flour

Dust work surface with flour, roll dough (and excess flour) out of bowl onto work surface.

Divide dough into 2 portions, then (one portion at a time) roll dough on work surface in flour to shape and place in pan.

Place pans in a warm draft-free location, cover with a lint-free towel, and proof for 30 minutes.

Before dough is fully proofed...

Move rack to middle of oven and pre-heat to 400 degrees F.

30 minutes later

When oven has come to temperature... place pans in oven and bake for 35 minutes.

35 minutes later

Gently turn loaf out on work surface and place on cooling rack.

Mexican Jalapeño-Chili Fiesta Bread (preheated uncovered baker)
Celebrate the flavors of a fiesta with this Jalapeño-Chili bread. If you like jalapeño and chilies... you'll love this loaf.

I used an *Emerson Creek Pottery* bread baking bowl (2-3/4" x 8") to shape this loaf. According to King Arthur Flour, "For best results, treat your stoneware pan with care. Oil your stoneware pan with neutral-flavored vegetable oil before each use; a nice patina will develop over time. For additional prevention of sticking, sprinkle a thin layer of cornmeal or semolina into the bottom of the oiled pan." And I agree with their suggestions, but I still had a problem with dough sticking. I found it best to preheat the bowl and spray it with no-stick spray until it was seasoned. That is why I am using the bread baking bowl as the example for "preheated covered baker".

Mexican Jalapeño-Chili Fiesta Bread

Pour warm water in a 3 to 4 qt warm glass mixing bowl (use a warm bowl... you don't want a cold bowl to take the heat out of the warm water).

12 oz warm Water

Add salt, yeast, chilies, peppers, corn, and olive oil... give a quick stir to combine.

1-1/2 tsp Salt
1-1/4 tsp Instant Yeast
2 whole Green Chilies (diced)
1/2 cup sliced Jalapeño Peppers
1/2 cup Golden Sweet Corn
1 Tbsp extra-virgin Olive Oil

Add flour... then cheese... stir until dough forms a shaggy ball, scrape dry flour from side of bowl, then tumble dough to combine moist flour with dry flour.

3-1/2 cups Bread Flour
3 slices Pepper Jack Cheese (diced)

Cover bowl with plastic wrap, place in a warm draft-free location, and proof for 1-1/2 hours.

1-1/2 hours later (preheated uncovered baker | baste)

When dough has risen and developed its gluten structure... spray an 8" proofing skillet with no-stick cooking spray and set aside.

"Degas, pull and stretch"... stick handle end of a plastic spoon in the dough and stir (dough will form a sticky ball). Then, scrape side of bowl to get remainder of the dough into the sticky dough ball.

Baste... drizzle dough and side of bowl with oil and roll-to-coat.

1 Tbsp Vegetable Oil

Roll dough out of bowl into proofing skillet.

Place skillet in a warm draft-free location, cover with a lint-free towel, and proof for 30 minutes.

Before dough is fully proofed...

Move rack to middle of oven, place baker in oven and pre-heat to 400 degrees F.

30 minutes later

When oven has come to temperature... remove baker from oven, transfer dough from proofing skillet to baker, shake to center, place baker back in oven and bake for 50 minutes (bake time was increased 10 minutes because peppers, chilies, corn, etc. added moisture which needs to bake out).

50 minutes later

Gently turn loaf out on work surface and place on cooling rack.

Buttermilk Bread (long covered baker)

If you like buttermilk ranch dressing... you'll like buttermilk bread. And this isn't the average buttermilk bread... this is an artisan loaf with an airy crumb and tender crust. The appearance is excellent... the taste is great. Buttermilk is a great all-purpose bread. Buttermilk gives it a rich tangy flavor with a subtle buttery depth that is great for sandwiches and toast.

It is a common misconception to associate buttermilk with the richness of butter but... buttermilk does not have butterfat. Buttermilk is the liquid remaining after taking the butter fat out of the milk in the process of making butter, thus it is lower in calories and fat than butter and higher in calcium, vitamin B12 and potassium than regular milk. And it's important to use cultured buttermilk, if you substitute 2% for cultured buttermilk in this recipe it will upset the balance of wet and dry ingredients (it's thinner), and you don't want to lose the nutritional value of buttermilk. After all, you wouldn't want to take the "yo" out of yogurt.

I used a *Sassafras* superstone oblong covered baker (13-1/2" x 4-1/2" x 2-1/2") to shape and bake this loaf because the crust of buttermilk bread has a tendency to turn dark brown and the cover will protect the crust... then I can control the color when I remove the cover to finish baking.

Buttermilk Bread

Pour buttermilk and water to a 3 to 4 qt glass mixing bowl and microwave on high for 1 minute.

8 oz Cultured Buttermilk
6 oz warm Water

Add salt, yeast, sugar and oil... give a quick stir to combine.

1-1/2 tsp Salt
1-1/4 tsp Instant Yeast
1 Tbsp Sugar
1 Tbsp Vegetable Oil

Add flour... stir until dough forms a shaggy ball, scrape dry flour from side of bowl, then tumble dough to combine moist flour with dry flour.

3-1/2 cups Bread Flour

Cover bowl with plastic wrap, place in a warm draft-free location, and proof for 1-1/2 hours.

1-1/2 hours later (long covered baker)

When dough has risen and developed its gluten structure... spray bottom of baker with no-stick spray and set aside.

"Degas, pull and stretch"... stick handle end of a plastic spoon in the dough and stir (dough will form a sticky ball). Then, scrape side of bowl to get remainder of the dough into the sticky dough ball.

Garnish... sprinkle dough ball and side of bowl with seeds and roll-to-coat.

2 Tbsp Sesame Seeds

"Roll-to-coat"... sprinkle dough ball and side of bowl with flour and roll-to-coat (dusting dough ball with flour will make it easier to handle and shape the dough for the baker).

2 Tbsp Bread Flour

Dust work surface with flour, roll dough (and excess flour) out of bowl onto work surface, roll dough on work surface in flour to shape, and place in baker.

Cover with lid, place in a warm draft-free location, and proof for 30 minutes.

Before dough is fully proofed...

Move rack to lower third of the oven and pre-heat to 400 degrees F (baker does not have to be preheated).

30 minutes later

When oven has come to temperature... place baker in oven and bake for 40 minutes with the top on.

40 minutes later

Take it out of the oven, remove top, and place back in the oven for 3 to 15 minutes to finish the crust... depending on how rustic (hard) you like your crust.

3 to 15 minutes later

Gently turn loaf out on work surface and place on cooling rack.

Cinnamon Raisin Bread (small bread pan)
Homemade fresh from the oven cinnamon raisin bread is a great way to start your day and when our guests stay overnight, my wife wants them to wake up to the aroma of fresh for the oven cinnamon raisin bread filling the house.

I used a *Good Cook* premium nonstick bread pan (8" x 4" x 2-1/4") to shape this loaf. Raisin bread is ideally suited for a smaller bread pan.

Cinnamon Raisin Bread

Pour warm water in a 3 to 4 qt warm glass mixing bowl (use a warm bowl... you don't want a cold bowl to take the heat out of the warm water).

14 oz warm Water

Add salt, yeast, sugar, and cinnamon... give a quick stir to combine with a flat whisk or fork (it will make it easier to combine the cinnamon).

1-1/2 tsp Salt
1-1/4 tsp Instant Yeast
2 Tbsp Brown Sugar
1 Tbsp ground Cinnamon

Add flour... then raisins. Stir until dough forms a shaggy ball, scrape dry flour from side of bowl, then tumble dough to combine moist flour with dry flour.

3 cups Bread Flour
1 cup Raisins

Cover bowl with plastic wrap, place in a warm draft-free location, and proof for 1-1/2 hours.

1-1/2 hours later (small bread pan)

When dough has risen and developed its gluten structure... spray an 8" x 4" bread pan with no-stick cooking spray and set aside.

"Degas, pull and stretch"... stick handle end of a plastic spoon in the dough and stir (dough will form a sticky ball). Then, scrape side of bowl to get remainder of the dough into the sticky dough ball.

Scrape dough out of bowl into bread pan.

Place pan in a warm draft-free location, cover with a lint-free towel, and proof for 30 minutes.

Before dough is fully proofed...

Move rack to middle of oven and pre-heat to 400 degrees F.

30 minutes later

When oven has come to temperature... place loaf pan in the oven and bake for 45 minutes (typically I would bake a standard 3 cup loaf in a 4" x 8" bread pan for 35 minutes, but raisin bread may need to be baked for an additional 5 to 10 minutes because of the moisture and density of the raisins).

45 minutes later

Gently turn loaf out on to the work surface and place on a cooling rack (cooling racks allow the bottom of the loaf to air dry).

Made in the USA
Middletown, DE
23 July 2020

13461576R00035